MRS STEINBERG
AND THE BYKER BOY

Michael Wilcox

MRS STEINBERG AND THE BYKER BOY

OBERON BOOKS
LONDON

First published in 2000 by Oberon Books Ltd.
(incorporating Absolute Classics)
521 Caledonian Road, London N7 9RH
Tel: 020 7607 3637 / Fax: 020 7607 3629

e-mail: oberon.books@btinternet.com

A catalogue record for this book is available from the British Library.

ISBN: 1 84002 172 1

Cover design: Andrzej Klimowski

Typography: Richard Doust

Back cover photograph: Fergus Greer

Printed in Great Britain by Antony Rowe Ltd., Reading.

Characters

MATTY
a teenager

PETER
a teenager

JANICE
middle aged

APRIL
middle aged

MRS STEINBERG
senior citizen

Mrs Steinberg and the Byker Boy was first performed at The Bush Theatre, London on 7 June 2000, with the following cast:

MATTY, Paul Nicholls

PETER, Aidan Meech

JANICE, Jane Wood

APRIL, Gay Soper

MRS STEINBERG, Miriam Karlin

Director, Natasha Betteridge

Designer, Geoff Rose

PART ONE

It's summer in the year 2000 and we're in the basement of the 'Red Flag Charity Shop' in North Shields, a few miles east of Newcastle-upon-Tyne in the far north of England. The space is full of charity shop donations in some sort of chaotic order. What makes it different from other charity shops are the old posters of Karl Marx and Lenin that are peeling off the walls. There are piles of large yellow plastic sacks full of unusable clothes for the rag man. There is also an old wind-up gramophone for playing 78 rpm records along with a box of records.

MATTY, a teenage boy, is patiently operating the steam iron, which looks like a hand-held vacuum cleaner, only steam drifts out of it. The second-hand clothes he is ironing are hung from a clothes frame, and he passes the iron over them like a scanner. He works slowly and with concentration and doesn't say a word. He has a badge on which says 'Andrew'.

JANICE bustles in with a couple of yellow rag bags and tosses them onto the pile.

JANICE: Rag man today. Found your badge okay? (*Staring at his badge.*) …Andrew? Got the hang of the steam press?

MATTY: Umm.

JANICE: I'm a good teacher, me! (*MATTY doesn't answer but looks at her.*) You a mouse or what?

APRIL bustles in with a box of books.

APRIL: More sodding books. Mostly religion…and one for you, Janice: 'Sex for the over sixties'.

JANICE: I'll give you bloody sex! Don't go showing that to Andrew, mind, he hasn't learnt to speak yet.

APRIL: Another Andrew? Hello, son.

JANICE: Peter's overslept again!

APRIL: No he hasn't. He phoned in sick. He's at the hospital.

JANICE: Hospital? Don't tell me…a knob transplant.

APRIL: (*To MATTY.*) Take no notice of her.

JANICE: That Peter's a dark horse. I've often wondered what he gets up to.

APRIL: No one's in the shop, mind.

JANICE: (*Leaving.*) My turn. So what did happen to young Romeo?

APRIL: Wouldn't say.

JANICE: Bloody men…tight arsed one minute, gob shites the next. Don't you agree, Andrew?

MATTY sniggers to himself and carries on ironing.

(*Leaving.*) That boy'll talk himself into an early grave! We'll soon have you all to ourselves…

APRIL: …with Peter in hospital…

JANICE: …and the boss away to Poland in the morning…

APRIL: …a lamb to the slaughter, I'd say…

JANICE: …but he does handle that steam iron like a veteran.

APRIL: Are you sure you're happy, pet?

MATTY: Aye.

JANICE: Ah! He spoke!

APRIL: Pick me up, someone!

JANICE: Fat chance, fart face!

APRIL: To work! To work!

JANICE: 'To work! To work!' Stop sounding like an owl on speed.

APRIL: Move your flabby arse, Janice! Two more boxes to come down.

JANICE: Right.

JANICE goes back to the shop.

APRIL: (*To MATTY.*) So…where do you come from, Andrew? Shields?

MATTY shakes his head.

Where, then?

MATTY: Byker.

APRIL: A Byker boy? (*MATTY nods.*) Almost one of us. Not far to travel. On work experience?

MATTY: Young Trainee.

APRIL: A YT! That's a first!

JANICE returns with more boxes of donations.

He's a Young Trainee!

JANICE: You'll be flush with cash, then.

MATTY: An extra ten pounds on my Job Seekers.

JANICE: Right! Drinks on you.

APRIL: That makes you the only sod getting paid round here!

JANICE: You better bloody earn it! Keep ironing. (*Referring to some ironed clothes.*) Are these priced?

APRIL: Aye.

JANICE takes them up to the shop.

You're making a good job of that, mind. Done it before?

MATTY: No!

APRIL: I'm April, by the way…as in 'fool' and 'shower'. Look… (*She shows him her name badge.*) …just in case you forget. Funny…the last boy was called Andrew. Now then…do you know about books? No? No…

JANICE: (*Shouting from the shop.*) April, man! Get your fanny up here!

APRIL: (*Leaving.*) That woman's got a mouth like a sewer!

MATTY stops his ironing and goes over to the wind-up gramophone. He plucks up courage and winds the handle a couple of times, starts and stops the motor. He hears someone coming and nips back to his steam iron.

APRIL enters and slings two more rag bags on the pile.

Boss's on the way in. Have you met her?

MATTY shakes his head.

Scary bitch…

APRIL leaves. MATTY fishes out some of the 78 rpm records to see what they are. When JANICE comes in with bags full of new donations, he nips back to his ironing.

JANICE: It never stops! Come and help sort through this lot, Andrew. (*She empties the contents of the bags. All sorts of things fall out.*) You may as well learn where things go. Books over there. Children's toys…far corner. Clothes…poo…watch yourself…filthy this…like nana's knickers…in that basket. Keep the best, chuck the rest! Nothing's too good for The Red Flag Shop. Bin that! Keep…keep…bin…keep. Get it?

MATTY: Aye.

JANICE: Don't look so worried.

MATTY: I'm not!

JANICE: I won't gobble you up…not on your first morning, at least! (*They work.*) Eeee…the silence is deafening me! You're allowed to have a bit of a crack, you know! What you saw on the tele…how the town's doing…who you shagged last night…usual small talk. Don't look at me like that! I stopped in, you dirty bugger…knackered from a rough weekend. Look at this! Just my luck! Action Man with his legs missing! Bin!

MATTY: You got me all wrong, Janice.

JANICE: I have?

MATTY: I'm a noisy bastard, me…

> *PETER, another teenage boy, enters. He's sporting a bruised cheek that will become a black eye and is looking for sympathy. He doesn't see MATTY and makes for JANICE.*

JANICE: Look who's landed! I thought you were at the clap clinic.

PETER: I may have a fractured skull, Janice.

JANICE: Balls! I bet they stuck a clapometer up your arse and it set off the fire alarm!

PETER: It hurts like buggery.

JANICE: You'll cope okay then. What happened?

PETER: This huge thug…a Sunderland supporter…just because I had my Newcastle top on…he belted us one.

JANICE: Never!

PETER: He downed us with one blow, Janice. Without warning. Then he ran…the coward. I'll get him, mind.

JANICE: You know who it was, Peter?

PETER: Not his name, like. But I'll know him if I see him. I'll nack him. I will. I'll rearrange his body parts.

JANICE: So his knob is where his nose used to be? And he has a bollock hanging tastefully from each ear? That sort of thing?

As she cuddles him, he sees MATTY ironing and realises it's the lad that gave him the black eye.

PETER: (*Alarmed.*) Ahhh…

JANICE: (*Mothering him.*) There…there…

PETER: Ahhhh!

JANICE: (*Running out of patience.*) Stop your moaning, you soft shite.

PETER points helplessly at MATTY, who flashes his steam iron up and down with extra vigor.

PETER: Who's that?

JANICE: Our new lad, Andrew. The fastest tongue south of Whitley Bay.

PETER: Tried it, have you?

MATTY: Has she shite!

JANICE: Andrew, make poor Peter a cup of coffee…and have one yourself. You'll wear that bloody steam iron out!

APRIL: (*Off.*) Janice, man, you foul mouthed slag! You're wanted in the shop! Now!

JANICE leaves the boys together.

PETER: You just stay where you are! And watch what you're doing with that thing!

MATTY switches off the steam iron and goes towards PETER, who backs off. But MATTY calms him down with his hands and gently touches PETER's bruise.

You fucking moron…

MATTY kisses the bruise.

Andrew…so that's what they call you…

MATTY: You can read?

PETER: The last lad was called Andrew.

MATTY: My proper name's Matty.

PETER: Matty?

MATTY: There isn't a Matty badge, so I'm 'Andrew'.

PETER: Do you realise I've been standing here for five minutes and you haven't hit us once?

MATTY kisses him gently.

MATTY: Shut your face. I'll make you coffee.

MATTY fills up the kettle, switches it on and prepares two mugs of coffee. He looks at PETER questioningly.

PETER: Milk and two sugars… (*MATTY waits for the rest.*) …please. Why did you hit us?

MATTY: (*Eyeing the gramophone.*) I love dancing…

PETER: So you belted us one?

MATTY: Do you like dancing, Peter?

PETER: Why hit us?

MATTY: You pressed the wrong button.

PETER: You spotted us off the train at Byker Metro. Trailed after us like a lost dog down to the Byker cottage. Flashed your dick like it's a circus act next to me in the pisser. Gobbled us in the lock-up like you missed your tea. Then you belt me in the eye!

MATTY: You called us a poof…

PETER: Why…not exactly…

MATTY: You said, 'What made you gay?'

PETER: And you whispered like a fucking snake, 'Who are you calling poof?' and then you hit us! Aye…that's right.

MATTY: All the lads in Byker are like me…

PETER: …really…

MATTY: …but Byker boys aren't poofs…none of us. Got it, you Shields twat?

PETER: If you say so, Matty.

MATTY: What were you doing on our patch anyway?

PETER: I was on an away day special. Tynemouth cottage is closed for repairs. Fancied a trip down Byker. Hopped on the Metro. There you were waiting for me like a randy shark.

MATTY: Bollocks! You minced off the metro, flashed your eyes at everything in trousers, skipped in and out of the puddles like you were singin' in the rain…half of Byker was following you to see if the rest of the show lived up to the overture. I just happened to be first in the queue. Now drink your coffee! Sorry about your face, like.

PETER: Still alive, aren't I?

MATTY: Won't do it again.

PETER: Promise?

MATTY: Promise.

PETER: Okay.

MATTY winds up the gramophone and fishes out a 78 record and plays it. It's a slow foxtrot.

MATTY: (*Taking PETER's hand.*) That's good! Come on…

PETER: No, man, Matty…

MATTY: Yes, you queer bastard…

PETER: Piss off!

MATTY: Please.

PETER: No!

MATTY dances a few steps on his own rather well, then takes off the record.

Where did you learn to dance?

MATTY: Wallsend…

PETER: Oh….

MATTY: (*Seeing the Karl Marx poster.*) He's staring at us. Who is he?

PETER: Karl Marx…according to old Mrs Steinberg.

MATTY: Who did he play for?

PETER: (*Affectionately.*) Shut your face, you bent bastard…

MATTY: I'm trying my best to say sorry, Peter.

MATTY throws his arms around PETER and they embrace. They do not notice that MRS STEINBERG, a senior citizen, has entered and is watching them. She is carrying various papers and folders to do with running the shop.

MRS STEINBERG: Girls…girls! Cheek to cheek on your first morning? (*She dumps her papers and bag.*)

PETER: Sorry, Mrs Steinberg.

MRS STEINBERG: What have you done to your face? Who are you? (*Reading the badge.*) 'Andrew'? God! I hope you're better than the last one.

PETER: His real name's Matty.

MRS STEINBERG: Take it off, then.

MATTY: Thank you.

MRS STEINBERG: A name is important.

MATTY takes it off.

I'm glad to have the chance to meet you before I go.

MATTY: Where are you off to, like?

PETER: It's always some commie country, isn't it Mrs S…

MRS STEINBERG: Poland tomorrow. And it isn't 'some commie country', if you don't mind.

PETER: She was born there…

MRS STEINBERG: Yes.

PETER: …a hell of a long time ago.

MATTY: I bet.

MRS STEINBERG: Don't remind me, Peter. Now…to business. I always give new staff a short talk about The Red Flag Charity Shop.

PETER: She does…

MRS STEINBERG: Peter, zip the lip and fix the usual, please. (*PETER makes her usual morning cup of coffee.*) Now… Matty… Who's that on the wall?

MATTY: Karl Marx.

MRS STEINBERG: Good God! That's a first. Do you know who he was?

MATTY: Did he manage… (*He sees PETER gesticulating wildly.*) No…wait a moment. (*Trying to get a clue from PETER's miming.*) One of the Marx brothers?

MRS STEINBERG: He was a great political philosopher…

MATTY: ...I knew that really...

MRS STEINBERG: ...who changed the course of history.

MATTY: Really?

PETER: (*Handing MRS STEINBERG her coffee.*) Show him your party card, Mrs S. She carries it everywhere... (*MRS STEINBERG shows MATTY her card. He studies it closely.*) ...like an organ donor. So if she gets run over by a bus, they'll know she's a commie when they get her to the mortuary.

MRS STEINBERG: All the money we make here goes to good socialist causes...

PETER: ...'both at home and abroad'...

MRS STEINBERG: Shut up, Peter... Each month I put a bulletin on the board showing how much we've taken and where the latest donations have gone.

PETER: (*Reading from the board.*) Easington Colliery Widows...two hundred and fifty pounds...*Médecin sans Frontières*...five hundred pounds. Chenoble leukemia victims...five hundred pounds. Good round sums, Mrs S...Rumanian orphans...five hundred pounds.

MRS STEINBERG: Get the idea? I take a broad view of what a 'socialist cause' actually is. If any of my staff...and that includes new staff, Matty...have suggestions about deserving causes, then they let me know and we can all discuss it. I'm less Stalinist than I used to be, so don't be frightened of your own ideas. However... I *am* in charge...

PETER: ...she likes to think so...

MRS STEINBERG: I've run this shop myself every day for more than thirty years. Now I've delegated some things to Janice and April. But I'm still the Red Flag boss... Okay?

MATTY: Ummm…

MRS STEINBERG: And you're on work experience?

PETER: He's a YT.

MRS STEINBERG: How did you manage that?

MATTY: I talked the job centre into it.

PETER: You signed the papers.

MRS STEINBERG: Did I?

PETER: He's getting loads of cash each week, unlike some of us.

MATTY: Ummm…

MRS STEINBERG: Ummm…

PETER: That's his favourite word…ummm…

MRS STEINBERG: Are you frightened of words, Matty?

MATTY: Not frightened of anything.

MRS STEINBERG: Do you read much?

MATTY: I can read.

MRS STEINBERG: But do you?

MATTY: Sometimes.

PETER: Try him out, Mrs S.

MRS STEINBERG picks out a paper back.

MRS STEINBERG: If you read that from cover to cover, you can keep it.

MATTY: *My Childhood* by Maxim Gorky.

PETER: Always something foreign.

MATTY: Thank you.

PETER: I wish you'd give us videos, not books.

MRS STEINBERG: Peter never reads anything.

PETER: What lies!

MRS STEINBERG: We've sold thousands of books over the years. Everything you can think of…from the trashiest novel to the most profound philosophy… often for little more than a few pence. Reading… talking…arguing…challenging with new ideas in your head. My advice is think your own thoughts, not someone else's.

JANICE: (*Off.*) Andrew! We need a man in the shop!

MRS STEINBERG: You go, Matty. No good sending Peter…

PETER: Cheeky old bag!

MATTY goes to the shop.

MRS STEINBERG: You'll get the other eye blacked in a minute…

PETER: …sorry…

MRS STEINBERG: …by me! You've been here quite a while.

PETER: Ages.

MRS STEINBERG: Happy?

PETER: Yep.

MRS STEINBERG: Well, behave yourself while I'm away.

PETER: Wish I was going away somewhere.

MRS STEINBERG: Where would you like to go?

PETER: Australia.

MRS STEINBERG: Why?

PETER: Seen it on the telly. Aussie lads are dead handsome and always have loads of cash. What will you do when you get to Poland?

MRS STEINBERG: See who's still alive…who's dead. Family matters. Haven't been back since 1989. Probably my last visit, Peter.

PETER puts his arms round her and kisses her gently. She pats his arm affectionately.

PETER: How long are you away for?

MRS STEINBERG: Five weeks and a day…

PETER: Five weeks and a day? That's forever, Mrs S.

MRS STEINBERG: Not quite forever… Now! Are all the priced books in the shop?

PETER: Most of them.

MRS STEINBERG: I want them in the shop now…

PETER: (*Gathering the books.*) Right.

MRS STEINBERG: …and I want to speak to April.

PETER: Right.

PETER leaves and MRS STEINBERG starts to sort through the accounts and bank statements that she has brought with her.

MATTY comes in with more donations.

MATTY: More junk. (*He sees the accounts.*)

MRS STEINBERG: Who says? What are you staring at? Mind your own business.

MATTY: Sorry. I'm dead interested in figures and money an' that.

MRS STEINBERG: I wish I was. I like to leave everything in order, so things can run smoothly.

MATTY: If you ever want someone to check through things, or sort things out, I'm good at it.

MRS STEINBERG: This is your first morning, young man. But thanks for the offer.

APRIL comes in.

APRIL: You want me?

MRS STEINBERG: Matty, go back to the shop, please.

MATTY leaves.

Have you anything to tell me?

APRIL: Like what?

MRS STEINBERG: How many years is it now?

APRIL: What is this?

MRS STEINBERG: I may be old, but I'm not stupid.

APRIL: Look! I've better things to do…

MRS STEINBERG: I've checked the figures…

APRIL: …pricing, an' that…

MRS STEINBERG: …It's all here, if you want to see for yourself.

APRIL: The money…that's your problem.

MRS STEINBERG: Where were you on Sunday morning?

APRIL: That's my business! You get us for free, for Christ's sake!

MRS STEINBERG: I was hoping to get this sorted out between us…privately…not too much blood on the floor before I leave.

APRIL: May I go now? (*She starts to leave.*)

MRS STEINBERG: If you do, don't come back…ever.

APRIL hesitates and sits down again.

Now…have you been taking money from the till again?

APRIL: You always suspect me first.

MRS STEINBERG: Have you?

APRIL: I always pay it back. You know that.

MRS STEINBERG: When did you last take…

APRIL: …borrow…

MRS STEINBERG: …borrow money from the till?

APRIL: Last Friday.

MRS STEINBERG: How much?

APRIL: Twenty pounds.

MRS STEINBERG: Have you paid it back ?

APRIL: No. I have to wait till my giro's cashed.

MRS STEINBERG: Have you any other money that's still owing?

APRIL: Not sure…

MRS STEINBERG: April?

APRIL: Don't think so.

MRS STEINBERG: In the past quarter, the difference between the till and the cash is one hundred and ninety-five pounds. Have you been borrowing money each week?

APRIL: I always pay it back, Mrs Steinberg.

MRS STEINBERG: So you've been a regular borrower?

APRIL: You don't pay us a penny.

MRS STEINBERG: Why didn't you leave an IOU in the till?

APRIL: Don't know.

MRS STEINBERG: I have told you about this before, haven't I?

APRIL: Aye...

MRS STEINBERG: And I told you not to do it.

APRIL: Aye. And what's all this about Sunday morning? That's Janice.

MRS STEINBERG: Ah...that's Janice?

APRIL: I'm not saying it is, like. But I know what you're on about...and it is...the shifty cow. You cannot trust that woman! And she's got a tongue like a serpent!

MRS STEINBERG: Thank you, April. That's all for the moment.

APRIL: Can I get back to work now?

MRS STEINBERG: How are you going to pay back the money you owe?

APRIL: I'll think of something. It's just twenty pounds, mind! Not two hundred!

MRS STEINBERG: If I can't trust my own staff, who can I trust?

PETER bursts in.

PETER: Rag man's here! Come on you lot! Shift yourselves! (*Shouting to MATTY in the shop.*) Matty, man!

APRIL: I'll get him.

PETER: (*Grabbing a couple of sacks off the pile.*) You best move yoursel', Mrs S.

MATTY enters.

Where you been, Matty man? Grab two of them and follow me!

MATTY does as he's told and follows. MRS STEINBERG tries to help by shifting some bags nearer the exit. PETER and MATTY race back and tumble over them.

Howay! She's trying to break wor necks! (*To MRS STEINBERG.*) Stay out the way, man Mrs. This is one for the lads. Price some books. Be useful.

MATTY and PETER grab two more sacks each and exit.

MRS STEINBERG: Janice! Come down, please.

JANICE: (*Off.*) I cannot!

MRS STEINBERG: April can cope!

JANICE: (*Off.*) There's hell on, man!

MATTY and PETER are back and off again.

MRS STEINBERG: Janice!

JANICE enters.

JANICE: Hell, man!

MRS STEINBERG: Sit over here out of the way.

PETER and MATTY are back in and out during the following scene. There are about fifty rag bags to shift in all.

Tell me about the Sunday morning scam.

JANICE: What's a scam?

MRS STEINBERG: Tell me about the stall at Tynemouth market.

JANICE: What stall?

MRS STEINBERG: Janice…

JANICE: Oh that stall…

MRS STEINBERG: Yes.

JANICE: Has that fat cow been telling tales again? I'll bust her bloody lip!

MRS STEINBERG: How long has this been going on?

JANICE: Why…a few months. It's good, like. Why shouldn't I have a stall? I need to get money somehow. Has someone shopped us to the dole man?

MRS STEINBERG: Not as far as I know.

JANICE: There's nothing nicked. What's the problem?

MRS STEINBERG: Most of the things you sell come from this charity shop.

JANICE: It's all paid for.

MRS STEINBERG: If staff buy goods, they must be entered in the book. (*Showing her the book.*) There's nothing here, is there? Is there?

JANICE: Ah, man! No one bothers with that. I bet you've never looked in the staff book for years.

MRS STEINBERG: But it's not just you buying goods, Janice. Tell me about your friend.

JANICE: What? Lesley?

MRS STEINBERG: Yes… (*Making a note of the name she's hearing for the first time.*) …Lesley.

JANICE: She does car boots an' that.

MRS STEINBERG: She knows the business.

JANICE: Oh aye…razor sharp, her.

MRS STEINBERG: And she buys goods from us?

JANICE: Aye. She's a good customer. Spends loads in here.

MRS STEINBERG: Goods that you've priced?

JANICE: Not just me.

MRS STEINBERG: …that she sells at a huge profit, with you, on her Sunday stall?

JANICE: So what? We always sell stuff too cheap here.

MRS STEINBERG: That's insider dealing, Janice.

JANICE: Is it really? Red Flag makes money. Lesley makes money.

MRS STEINBERG: And so do you.

JANICE: So what? I work here for nothing, remember? Without me and the fat cow upstairs, you'd have closed years ago. Sorry to be blunt, like.

MRS STEINBERG: No need to apologise. Dealers come into the shop to make money. They know more than we do about the market value of what we sell. And I don't like them! I kick them out if I see one. We sell second-hand goods to people who need them…for themselves… for their own lives. We price things cheap enough for ordinary, working class people to afford. That's part of what Red Flag stands for. So no dealers and no dealer prices! And definitely no Lesley! If you want to go into business, work somewhere else.

PETER and MATTY only have two or three more trips to go. They've been listening to bits of the conversation and have got the gist of what it's about.

PETER: (*Interrupting.*) Donations flooding in upstairs! Mad day, this.

He leaves with MATTY.

JANICE: And I don't like being tret like a bairn!

MRS STEINBERG: I'm trying to treat you like an adult.

JANICE: Just get real, Mrs Steinberg. When you started up, maybes you were the only Charity Shop in North Shields. But now we're over run with them, and in Byker and Wallsend and Whitley Bay. They're everywhere. It's not socialism that's taking over the world, it's bloody Charity Shops! And car boots and markets. If it carries on like this, no one will ever buy anything from new ever again! Face the facts! We're all grafters and scavengers. For the past thirty-five years you've lead the charge, Mrs Steinberg, but you're running out of steam.

MRS STEINBERG: We're making money out of nothing, passing on that money where it does some good to the working classes, and harming no one in the process.

JANICE: Putting half the traders in the town out of business…

MRS STEINBERG: …not us…

JANICE: …and screwing the tax man till he weeps!

MRS STEINBERG: I don't think either of us need lose sleep over that.

PETER enters with bags of donations.

PETER: There's more upstairs. Your lucky day, Mrs S.

APRIL: (*Off.*) Janice, man, you're wanted!

JANICE: (*Shouting back.*) I'm busy!

APRIL: (*Off.*) Janice!

JANICE: (*Shouting back.*) My legs are tied together!

APRIL: (*Off.*) Use your crows feet and hop up!

JANICE: (*To MRS STEINBERG.*) She's such a sly bitch! I bet she wants a fag out the back.

JANICE leaves.

MRS STEINBERG: (*Wearily.*) What am I going to do, Peter?

PETER: Don't know, Mrs S. Would you like a neck massage?

MRS STEINBERG: Is there anything you don't do?

PETER: Duck when someone throws a punch.

MRS STEINBERG: I've had the same problem several times in my life.

PETER massages MRS STEINBERG temples and neck.

What shall I do? What shall I do?

PETER: That's what I said when I left school. I ended up here.

MRS STEINBERG: Are we really doing any good? Is it worth the effort?

PETER: We helped pay for the old people's day out. That was good. We sent money to…what was that mad business?

MRS STEINBERG: Cuba.

PETER: That's the one. Cuba.

MRS STEINBERG: We didn't send money. We sent pencils.

PETER: Pencils to Cuba…how many did we send?

MRS STEINBERG: Ten thousand. It seemed a good idea at the time.

PETER: Surely they had enough pencils already, Mrs S?

MRS STEINBERG: It was a long time ago, Peter. I read an article…in Tribune, I think it was. Got the idea. Grabbed the phone. Did a deal with the suppliers. Wrote a cheque and Hey Presto! The pencils were dispatched within the week.

PETER: Did anyone write back?

MRS STEINBERG: No. I never heard another word.

PETER: Were people any worse off there than we were here?

MRS STEINBERG: That's not quite the point. I just think that when you send money…or pencils even…out of the blue, across the world, and for no obvious personal gain, that's making a useful statement.

PETER: If things don't get nicked at the other end. Or if people don't hijack our money and pretend they gave it themselves.

MRS STEINBERG: That's cynical, Peter.

PETER: That's reality, Mrs S. People are like that.

MRS STEINBERG: Thirty years ago, there was a clear 'them' and 'us' in the world. At least, I thought so. 'The Red Flag Charity' meant something. Now, everything's out of focus. The pigs have been walking on their hind legs so long, even I can't tell the difference.

PETER: Don't worry, Mrs S. You've still got your party card.

MRS STEINBERG: Yes, I have…a small piece of history…a collector's item. I've been stopped in the street so people can have a look at it. It's become my most famous possession. And now I'm wondering whether it's the longest running, worst joke ever.

PETER: Have you ever thought of turning this place into a joke shop? I mean…you've got the staff…

JANICE and APRIL enter.

JANICE: What's this cow been saying behind my back?

APRIL: Ah, man! Hold your tongue!

JANICE: I warned you! I'll stick up for myself.

APRIL: You, you walking ulcer! You're just as bad.

MRS STEINBERG: Who's minding the shop?

JANICE: Don't panic! There's a lull.

APRIL: We've only taken ten pounds this morning.

JANICE: Plenty of donations.

APRIL: No cash.

PETER: Matty's on.

MRS STEINBERG: Not on his first morning, he isn't.

JANICE: He won't bugger the till.

PETER: Like a bet?

MRS STEINBERG: I'll go. Peter, are those books priced?

PETER: Aye.

MRS STEINBERG: Bring them up, please. You two, take a break, and stop bitching.

MRS STEINBERG leaves. PETER follows her with the newly-priced books.

JANICE: Can you believe the no smoking rule?
I'm gasping.

APRIL: I drink that much coffee working here, I'm North Shields number one hyperactive pisser.

JANICE: You shouldn't have split on us, mind.

APRIL: She knew already. Anyway, why shouldn't you make some money on a Sunday?

JANICE: That's what I told her. So what did you get wronged for?

APRIL: Nicking from the till.

JANICE: Not again…

APRIL: I only borrowed ten pounds till Friday.

JANICE: Twenty, I heard. It's a wonder there's anything left in the bloody till with so many thieves about. Eeee…do you want to know the truth about Saturday?

APRIL: Gan on…

JANICE: I had the best shag of my life. I did! It was stupendous!

APRIL: I couldn't cope with a stupendous shag.

JANICE: On Saturday night, I heard the angels sing. The lights on my Christmas tree were twinkling for hours afterwards.

APRIL: Was it some fellow, or was it that Lesley from the market stall?

JANICE: Do you mind! Smelly pants Lesley? God! You'd have to scrub her with brillo pads to get the muck off! With her you'd get lost in the undergrowth and never find your way out. She's got a cunt the size of Marsden Grotto. And in her case, the hairs on her dicky-divo really do hang down to her knees. Last year the whole street clubbed together to buy her a hedge trimmer. I'd get more pleasure sticking my tongue in a door mat!

APRIL: Who was it, then?

JANICE: A traffic warden from Cramlington. Now that doesn't sound too promising, I'll admit. But when you peal away the uniform and bin the parking tickets, what a huge and versatile dick! I'm telling you! He played Bach's Toccata and Fugue on my fallopian tubes! Then, for an encore, it was 'The Flight of the Bumble Bee' up my arse! I was screaming the house down. Mrs Green down below almost called the police. 'Are you alreet, Janice?' 'Course I'm alright! I'm getting the shag of a lifetime, you daft bat!'

APRIL: I thought you were walking a bit strange this morning.

JANICE: Walking strange?

APRIL: Like you still had a carrot…

JANICE: A carrot? Speak for yourself! Mr Cramlington had a cross between an aubergine and a cucumber!

APRIL: You mean his bell-end is like a colossal black currant?

PETER sticks his head round the door.

PETER: Mrs S says you're a couple of gob shites and would you sort out the donations?

PETER leaves.

JANICE: That one's got a prick the size of a cocktail sausage and balls like two garden peas! Come on, lover, let's see what's worth nicking.

They start to sort.

APRIL: *Patience Strong…*

JANICE: …nights in the garden of Lesbos…

APRIL: A spinning top.

JANICE: I want a go. Please, please, please!

The top hums.

APRIL: Eeee! That's lovely. Little Michael would just love that.

JANICE: Who's Little Michael?

APRIL: No one's quite sure. But he lives next door and the whole street loves him.

JANICE: Stick it in with the rest of the sex toys.

APRIL: Bin…bin…save…rag bag…

JANICE: Rag bag…rag bag…rag bag…

APRIL pulls a dead, skinned cat, with a ligature round its neck, out of a black bin liner.

APRIL: Ahhh!

She drops it and reels with shock.

JANICE: Oh my God! What a stink!

APRIL: It's a baby! It's a baby!

JANICE: Oh no… Oh Jesus!

APRIL: Ahhhh…

PETER comes in to see what's happening.

It's a baby!

PETER: Ohhhh…

PETER throws up.

MATTY enters.

APRIL: I'm feeling faint.

PETER: Get a man…get a man…

JANICE: You are a man, you twat!

MATTY: It's a cat. It's a dead cat. Some bugger's skinned it.

JANICE: Deal with it, Andrew.

MATTY: I'll take it out to the skip. And stop calling me Andrew!

MATTY picks it up and stuffs it into a bag and takes it out.

JANICE: You're a fine pair in a crisis.

APRIL: I'd like to skin the bastard who did that to us.

PETER: I'd like to put a rope around his bloody neck.

JANICE: It was a her. I was there when she came.

PETER: Who?

APRIL: Not your Lesley?

JANICE: No. This old biddy. Never seen her before.
The bitch…

MATTY returns.

MATTY: All gone.

JANICE: Not quite. The bent cow brought that other bin
liner an' all. Do you remember that time someone
donated a sack of dead rabbits?

PETER: (*To APRIL.*) You okay?

APRIL: I'm shaking, me.

PETER: I'll get you some water.

JANICE: She likes something stronger, her.

MATTY looks in the other bin liner.

MATTY: Looks like old clothes.

JANICE: Rag bag, rag bag, rag bag the lot of them!

MATTY: And…hang on…

APRIL: Oh no…

PETER: Do it outside, Matty man!

JANICE: I want to see!

MATTY pulls out a carrier bag. He looks in and recoils.

MATTY: Ah man! It's full of shite!

PETER: Never!

MATTY: It is!

PETER: Let's have a look.

JANICE: We've had that before an'all.

APRIL: A dead cat and a bag of shite?

JANICE: That should advance the cause of world revolution.

MATTY: Do you not want a look, like?

APRIL: No!

PETER: Just a little look?

APRIL: Take it out of here!

MATTY takes it out to the skip.

PETER: What did she look like?

JANICE: Old and daft-looking. She smelt like a tom cat.

PETER: Maybe she was just doing a bit of spring cleaning.

APRIL: You remember old Millie? She used to wrap her shite in newspaper like it was fish and chips and dump it all over town. It's true. She walked miles every day whatever the weather. In the end a big gust of wind blew her in front of a 37 bus. She was squashed flat.

PETER: What happened to her bag?

APRIL: They say the police took it away to give to her next of kin…

PETER/JANICE Uuurghhh…

MATTY comes back.

MATTY: I never knew work could be so much fun.

JANICE: Just an average sort of morning.

APRIL: Wait till you've been here a week.

MATTY: Mrs Thingy wants you two upstairs.

APRIL: Mrs Thingy…

MATTY: Says she's got to go out.

JANICE: Typical boss. Cause chaos and then bugger off for
lunch. (*To APRIL.*) Come on, lover. Fresh air'll do you
good. Carry on sorting, you two.

*They leave MATTY and PETER together. PETER starts
sorting. MATTY is more interested in the accounts and bank
books that MRS STEINBERG has left behind.*

PETER: So what's with Wallsend and dancing?

MATTY: My mam loves line dancing. I went along for a
laugh and got hooked on another class they had. It was a
great way of keeping away from Da.

PETER: Oh.

MATTY: Then mam started having this affair with a sheriff
with a stuck on moustache. They chat each other up like
she's a cowgirl and he's a gunslinger with a badge. Quite
sickening, really.

PETER: What about your da?

MATTY: Beats the shit out of us. Evil bastard. Beats up
mam, an'all. (*MATTY notes a few numbers from the files.*)

PETER: Has he got a job?

MATTY: Aye. He's a postman. Wyatt Earp's planning to
gun him down while he's doing the second delivery.
What about you?

PETER: I live with my mam. Da has another family in the
West End. Don't see much of him. Mam works in a café.

Me Nana lives down the street and keeps things straight.
They share the same bloke.

MATTY: How old's your Nana?

PETER: Fifty something.

MATTY: How does that work?

PETER: He's with Nana on a Monday and a Wednesday,
and mam on a Tuesday and a Friday.

MATTY: What's he do at the weekends?

PETER: Gans out wi' the lads.

MATTY: Does your mam know what's gannin' on with your
Nana an' that?

PETER: Oh aye. The whole street knows. Everyone's okay
about it. Not a problem. Are you going to help me or what?

MATTY: Just a minute. (*He finds two bank cards. He checks the
dates and sees that they overlap, making both cards valid.*)
Nice one! (*He pockets one and slips the other back.*)

PETER: What are you playing at?

MATTY: Nothing. (*Finding something.*) Where does this gan?

PETER: O'er there.

MATTY: Does anyone ever buy these old records?

PETER: Hardly ever. They'll end up getting binned.

MATTY: I wouldn't mind them…and this. (*He means the
wind-up gramophone.*)

PETER: Ask Janice. Offer her a pound for the lot.

MATTY: Can I?

PETER: Yep.

MATTY: Come out with me tonight?

PETER: What for?

MATTY: Fun.

PETER: On a date?

MATTY: Yes.

PETER: I was thinking I might give my bruise a rest.

MATTY: Why, man, that's nawt. Wait till you meet me da.

PETER: Where to, like?

MATTY: I could take you to the dancing.

PETER: What!

MATTY: I could.

PETER: In Wallsend?

MATTY: Aye.

PETER: I bet you and me would be the only lads…with loads of spotty lasses.

MATTY: There's spotty lads as well.

PETER: No, man. I'm not gannin' there.

MATTY: It's not at all what you think. Anyway, if we don't like it, we don't have to stay. We could go into the town after.

PETER: Clubbing?

MATTY: Free for us on a Monday.

PETER: Which club?

MATTY: Power House? Rockshots? Whatever you want. We can dance together. No hassle. Better than Byker cottage.

PETER: Got nee coin.

MATTY: Me neither.

PETER: Okay. We'll gan.

MATTY: Good.

PETER: Aye…

JANICE: (*Off.*) Peter, man!

PETER: That woman never gets off your back.

MATTY: Me neither…

PETER: (*To MATTY.*) Cheeky slut! (*Shouting upstairs.*) What?

JANICE: More donations!

PETER: (*To MATTY.*) Shields has gone mad!

MATTY: (*Referring to the steam iron.*) Can I do this?

PETER: Aye.

> *PETER leaves and MATTY gets the steam iron going and sorts out some dresses, one of which he checks out against himself, and dances with.*
>
> *PETER comes back with more boxes of donations.*

That's about a month's worth in a morning…

MATTY: …so far…

PETER: I think you're jinxed.

MATTY: That's what Da says. I'm bad luck. I'm responsible for everything that's wrong in the world. He says he cannot even remember shagging Mam to have us.

PETER: Maybe your real da was an alien…or a cowboy. You really like that steam iron…

MATTY: …aye…

PETER: I was always jealous of the other boys at school…when their fathers turned up to watch them playing football…or took them on trips to see things.

MATTY: I'm jealous of you not having one. Mine's made our lives hell from day one. That's him that hit you last night…the effect he's had on me. Everyone thinks I'm a real hard lad 'cos I used to gan round belting people twice my size. I'd hate people to know how much I love sucking cocks.

PETER: When did you start, like?

MATTY: This lad bought some of his Star War toys to the middle school.

PETER: Oh…

MATTY: We started playing on with them. One thing led to another and I sucked his cock in the bogs. So I blame Harrison Ford.

APRIL enters.

APRIL: Janice says you two are either slacking or shagging, so I've come down to check…

PETER/MATTY: We're shagging.

APRIL: (*Shouting upstairs.*) They're shagging!

PETER: Matty's Queen of the Steam Iron.

APRIL: You two don't waste much time, considering you've only just met.

PETER: We're hot lads. What do you expect?

APRIL: If all the lads had shagged each other instead of me, my life would have been a hell of a lot better.

PETER finds some cups and saucers each wrapped in tissue.

PETER: These are smart.

APRIL: How many are there?

PETER: Whole bagful…

APRIL: Janice'll have them for the stall. Stick'em o'er there, pet. Not where you threw up! There!

MATTY: 'Get a man…get a man!'

PETER: Shut your face!

APRIL: Eeee…that poor cat! I'll never eat for a week. Reminded me of my first bairn.

PETER: Is that Freddie the fish? (*To MATTY.*) He's a chippy.

APRIL: Freddie? He was my third, man, Peter! My first was John the robber. I was fifteen and didn't dare tell me mam what was happening. No one knew I was pregnant. They thought it was puppy fat. At school I walked about with a lassie on each arm in case the lads bumped into us. Everyone thought I was a dyke. One day I went home at lunchtime, felt funny, and had the baby on the kitchen floor.

PETER: On your own?

APRIL: Aye…what a bloody mess! Me mam came back and saw us lying there with blood and muck everywhere. She thought I'd been murdered. Then baby John started his screaming and she passed right out! Splat! Onto the floor herself. Messy business.

PETER: So he's a robber?

APRIL: That's just his nickname. When he was a lad, he tackled these crooks who were robbing the Abbey National. Police arrested him, of course, before they realised he wasn't one of the robbers.

PETER: So what's he do now?

APRIL: John? He's a catholic priest in London. Wouldn't surprise me if he was the Pope one day. Still be John the robber to us, mind.

PETER: Matty wants the gramophone…

MATTY: …and the records…

APRIL: Oh aye…

MATTY fishes out a record and plays it.

Let's see you dance. (*PETER takes her hand.*) Not me. You two.

JANICE and MRS STEINBERG enter.

MATTY stops the music.

MRS STEINBERG: Sorry. The party's over.

APRIL: Who's minding the shop?

JANICE: Shurrup, man…we've locked the door.

PETER: (*To MATTY.*) Something's up…watch yoursel'…

APRIL: It's her end of term speech…

MRS STEINBERG: Is it worth it any more?

APRIL: Who are you asking?

MRS STEINBERG: All of you, damn it! You are loyal… and I'm grateful for that…but you're also a bunch of bloody thieves and con men…

MATTY: …I've only been here a couple of hours…

PETER: Ssshhh…

MRS STEINBERG: …and I can't take any more of it. You realise I own this damn shop? And there are people wanting to buy it? Developers. Urban renewal money.

You've seen what they've done to the Fish Quay?
They've not finished yet!

JANICE: You swore you'd never sell.

MRS STEINBERG: I know…

APRIL: …well, then…

MRS STEINBERG: …things change…and you're all
ripping me off…

PETER: …not me…

MRS STEINBERG: …and, bluntly, I have had my bellyful
of the lot of you! The Red Flag Shop was never a game.
Not to me. In an average week, we can make over three
hundred pounds. We once made over five hundred
pounds.

JANICE: Once…

MRS STEINBERG: All the facts and figures of the last
thirty-five years are there… (*Meaning the books she left on
the table.*) …and you're free to inspect them while I'm
away if you want to find out what we're really all about.
Every donation we ever made…how much and who to.
I know some of my work has misfired…pencils to Cuba,
Peter…but most of it hasn't.

APRIL: You've made a lot of people happy, Mrs S.

JANICE: Arse licker!

MRS STEINBERG: The heart of this shop has always been
in the right place. I never expected you to share my
particular view of the world, but we don't exist to steal
from each other…to lie…to cheat…to put number one
first. Frankly, I'm both proud…and ashamed of the lot
of you!

MATTY: Even me, Mrs?

JANICE: Mrs…

MRS STEINBERG: Shut up, Janice! I'm trusting you all to run the shop while I'm away. Make any changes you want. Do what you think is best. But keep the books up to date…and, if you wish, make a list of all the donations you'd like me to make on my return. If I come back to find everything in chaos, I'll close the shop and sell up…at once. Is that clear? (*Silence.*) Convince me that the party isn't over…if you can. I'll see you…how long, Peter?

PETER: Five weeks and day… Have a lovely time, Mrs S.

APRIL: Bring us back some pressies.

MRS STEINBERG: We'll see…

JANICE: No late nights or loose living.

MRS STEINBERG: (*Gathering up her things.*) Shut your face.

PETER: And keep off the booze.

MRS STEINBERG: Fat chance.

JANICE: So who's the boss?

APRIL: Someone's got to be in charge.

MRS STEINBERG: You're a collective. Behave!

She leaves.

MATTY: What's a collective?

PETER: One of those commie things.

JANICE: It means if I say move your arse, you move!

APRIL: It means we're all equal.

JANICE: Does it shite…

MATTY: I'll do the books.

PETER: Clever him, you know.

MATTY: (*To JANICE and APRIL.*) You two, get the shop open again. We can't make money with the door locked.

JANICE: Who said you could give the orders, Byker boy?

MATTY: Howay! Let's all use wor heads for once. We've got loads of time…

PETER: Tell 'em, Matty!

MATTY: …let's make a go of it.

APRIL: He is a YT, Janice.

JANICE: YT? Young tart!

MATTY: Move your arse, Janice!

JANICE: Don't you order my arse around!

APRIL: Come on! Let's open for business.

JANICE: (*To MATTY as she leaves with APRIL.*) I'm watching you, dick head!

MATTY prepares the gramophone.

MATTY: You're going to dance with me.

PETER: Tonight.

MATTY: Now.

PETER: Am I shite.

MATTY: Do what you're told or I'll slap you one.

PETER: Oooooooo!

The music starts.

MATTY: Come on…

PETER: Na!

MATTY: Matty wants his lover boy.

MATTY takes PETER's hand and they dance, with PETER increasingly intimate with MATTY, who is forceful but gentle with him.

End of Part One.

PART TWO

Five weeks and a day later.

The basement of the charity shop has undergone a remarkable change. It has been thoroughly cleaned and organised. The posters of Marx and Lenin have been steamed off the walls, and are now rolled up neatly, awaiting MRS STEINBERG's return. The whole impression is of a well-run business. There are charts and graphs on the walls, and an easel with paper and felt tip pens for training and brain storming.

MATTY is working away at a newly-installed computer, checking something out on the internet. Not everything is going well.

MATTY: (*Frustrated by the machine.*) Damn! Come on!

> *He is better turned out than before, with clean, fashionable clothes and tidy hair.*

> (*He types in a programme he's just created, and enters it.*) Yes! Gotcha!

> *He sits back while the machine does the work. He plays music on the computer's sound system, in contrast to the previous wind up gramophone. He types in a response and rubs his hands in excitement as things go according to plan, for the moment.*

> *Inspite of his outward appearance, he is concealing some bruising on his body and is in some pain.*

> *PETER enters with overalls, a tin of paint and a brush.*

We don't want that down here.

PETER: You've been too bossy lately. You know that?

MATTY: Paint goes in the new furniture store.

PETER: Yes, sir…by the way, boss, this *is* a collective, in case you've forgotten.

An e-mail comes through on the computer. MATTY turns off the music and PETER puts down the paint and brush to watch.

Any luck?

MATTY: How does ninety-five pounds sound?

PETER: Good.

MATTY: There's Mr Faithful in America to come back to us.

PETER: Is he offering more?

MATTY: Might do.

PETER: Nice one.

MATTY: Even in a collective, whatever that is, someone has to make decisions eventually. Have they finished upstairs?

PETER: Almost. We've got the best part of an hour. Janice has persuaded Lesley to pin down Mrs Steinberg at home.

MATTY: Sounds like fun.

PETER: Her flight was on time into Newcastle, apparently.

MATTY: (*Referring to something on the screen.*) Look at this…we had a copy of that. Guess what we sold it for…

PETER: Fifty pence.

MATTY: A pound. This bloke's selling it for two hundred and fifty pounds!

PETER: Dealer?

MATTY: Collector having a clear out, I reckon. Add him to our list… (*MATTY types in the details and saves them.*)

MATTY stretches with tiredness in front of the screen. PETER bends down and kisses him affectionately.

If you get paint on me…

PETER: I won't. God! You're in bad fettle today.

MATTY: Sorry.

PETER: Too many late nights. Bad boy…

MATTY: Rockshots was good…

PETER: Did you have to enter the sexy nipple contest?

MATTY: I've got great tits.

PETER: I hated it when that poxy wanker started licking them.

MATTY: They're on special offer this week. Now will you get back to work?

PETER: Next week it'll be your arse, no doubt.

MATTY: (*Springing to his feet and twisting PETER's arm viciously.*) Who won the Mr Pansy competition?

PETER: Ahhhh! That hurts, Matty!

JANICE enters, unseen by the lads.

MATTY: Who? Who?

PETER: Me! Me! Me!

JANICE grabs the pair them by the scruffs of their necks.

JANICE: Kiss and make up! (*Shoves them roughly together then drags them apart.*)

PETER: (*To MATTY.*) I'll not forget that!

JANICE: Now piss off the pair of you and get some work done! (*She shoves them apart.*)

MATTY: (*To PETER.*) Slack arsed git!

JANICE: We've worked our fingers to the bone for a month, and I'm not going to see everything mucked up by a couple of nancy boys! Peter get your cheesy knob upstairs. And send down the April shower.

PETER: Into water sports, Janice?

JANICE: Piss off!

PETER: She's into everything!

JANICE: And clean yourself up, you tart!

PETER grabs his paint and brush and races away.

MATTY: Banged your eye, Janice?

JANICE: Why?

MATTY: Looks a bit red.

JANICE: Walked into a door.

MATTY: Bit of rough, more like.

JANICE: You should know, dickhead. Have you done your homework?

MATTY: Everything's ready.

APRIL enters.

APRIL: Just sold that pram for a tenner!

MATTY: Should we sell condoms and sachets of Liquid Silk?

APRIL: Not much demand for second hand blobs, Matty.

MATTY: From new, you moron.

JANICE: Not bloody likely! You and randy Peter would be permanently joined at the hip!

APRIL: What've you done to your eye?

JANICE: Don't you start!

APRIL: Let me guess… Mr Aubergine from Cramlington turned round too fast and you forgot to duck?

JANICE: If Mr Aubergine turned round too fast, he'd take off like a helicopter!

APRIL: The paint round the shop window still isn't dry.

JANICE: Don't touch it, then! God! We've done all we could.

APRIL: I'm not sure Mrs Steinberg will be pleased we've taken out a lease on the shop next door.

JANICE: It isn't 'we'. I've done it. With the money we're getting from our 'reasonable expenses'. Anyway, now we collect donations, we need somewhere to store everything.

APRIL: There's more to it than that. I reckon you're scheming something. Sly bitch!

JANICE: Stop overloading your brain. Just be grateful.

MATTY: No more lugging bags upstairs for the rag man, April.

APRIL: I know that. I still think that sweaty cow's up to something.

JANICE: Doesn't our new boy look sweet? So neat and clean. A right little businessman. (*She smacks him one.*) Tosser!

MATTY: (*Looking at the screen.*) Hang on! Old Faithful's up late! Damn! He doesn't want the Dore Bible…but…yes! three hundred dollars for Livingstone's 'Missionary Travels' first edition! (*He types fluently.*) More goodies to come from that collection, Mr Faithful…as you will eventually find out…

APRIL: I still don't know where you learnt all that computer stuff.

MATTY: School…a friend's house…then got one at home…

JANICE: Don't distract him. The boy's a genius. Matty, keep making money. April, pet, before the balloon goes up…

APRIL: What balloon?

JANICE: You've been here the longest, so I thought we better talk. How many years is it?

APRIL: Almost twenty.

JANICE: Blood is thicker than water…

APRIL: What the fuck are you on about?

MATTY: (*Having trouble with the computer.*) Shit! (*He checks out the cables at the back of the machine.*)

JANICE: I suppose that's why the old bitch hasn't sacked you.

APRIL: What for?

JANICE: You're still nicking from the till, you bent cow!

APRIL: What lies!

JANICE: (*She goes to the easel.*) When we launched New Red Flag four weeks ago, we all made an agreement. (*She whips back the paper to reveal a previous training lecture.*) We were going to turn a clapped out, corrupt business…

APRIL: …back to school…

JANICE: …which was failing dismally to capitalise on its assets, into something that worked and made loads of cash!

APRIL: God! You're even worse than that little shit! (*Meaning MATTY.*)

JANICE: …and thanks to hard graft, imagination, a bit a streetwise business sense and the boy wonder here, we've transformed ourselves into North Shields's top charity shop!

MATTY: No one's to come near the computer, right?

JANICE: (*Ignoring him.*) Everyone's talking about New Red Flag. All the big charities, who used to spit in our eyes as we passed, are now beating a path to our door to see how we're doing it! But what do you do, you syphilitic bitch?

APRIL: Which syphilitic bitch are you talking to? I can see three…

JANICE: You just carry on in the same old way, helping yourself when you're short…

APRIL: I always pay it back when the giro comes through.

JANICE: Do you fuck! You're not talking to a senile old biddy, Miss Smarty-Pants!

APRIL: You're not exactly Miss Skidmark-Free-Zone yourself!

JANICE: I bloody am! I'm a reformed character!

APRIL: Not so reformed that you've stopped selling New Red Flag property with your gorilla friend on a Sunday!

JANICE: Tell her, Matty! Tell her the truth.

MATTY: Tynemouth market is all part of New Red Flag business now. It's all correctly accounted for.

APRIL: '…all correctly accounted for…' Give me a gun, someone!

MATTY holds up the balance sheet to prove his point.

JANICE: So how much did you nick last week, April?

APRIL: Ten pounds.

MATTY: Fifteen pounds, actually.

JANICE: And the week before?

APRIL: I don't remember.

MATTY: Twenty pounds.

APRIL: Never in the world!

MATTY: Fifteen pounds on the Monday and five pounds on Thursday.

MATTY prints out the details and passes the sheet to APRIL.

APRIL: Jesus wept…it's like the bloody secret police!

MATTY: That's what you owe from the last three weeks. There were more important programmes to write in week one.

JANICE: Total?

MATTY: Sixty-five pounds…plus whatever it was in the first week of new trading.

JANICE: So what are you going to do about it, you manky pussy?

APRIL: Don't look at me. I've got nee coin.

JANICE: Matty?

MATTY: No expenses for you, April. And no productivity dividend at the end of the month until it's all paid back. Every penny.

JANICE: Or, if you prefer, you can fuck off out of here for good.

MATTY: Or call the coppers?

JANICE: Not bloody likely!

APRIL: Typical man! All snitch and no snatch!

MATTY: Better than being all snatch!

JANICE: We'll handle things ourselves, even if we have to knee-cap the bitch!

APRIL: (*To MATTY.*) Don't sit there with that smug face, cock sucker! Your turn will come. (*To JANICE.*) And so will yours, you shitty arsed shag bag!

APRIL storms back to the shop.

MATTY: Well, I'm glad our new, corporate image hasn't changed everything.

JANICE: Are you planning to jump ship?

MATTY: Not yet.

JANICE: But it is in your mind?

MATTY: I'm not going to spend the rest of my life as a minion in a charity shop. Anyway, with our revised expenses and bonus scheme, on top of my YT money, I'm not doing too badly at the moment.

JANICE: What if Mrs Steinberg tells us all to get stuffed?

MATTY: Wait till she sees the figures.

JANICE: She won't believe them.

MATTY: Everything's here. Can't argue with the facts.

JANICE: She can.

MATTY: Anyway, it's you that's most likely to bugger off.

JANICE: You reckon?

MATTY: Aye?

JANICE: Why, like?

MATTY: You and lethal Lesley…

JANICE: Oh aye…

MATTY: …market queens…you could operate five days a week.

JANICE: We do. She runs the stall. I scout for goods to sell.

MATTY: Stone age, Janice. (*Referring to the computer.*) This is where the serious money is…

JANICE: …if you've got serious junk to sell. Most of our stuff's crap.

MATTY: Even crap fetches good prices on the internet.

JANICE: Christ! What's the time? She'll be here in twenty minutes. Have a last check around down here. I'm going to tidy the furniture store.

MATTY: Send Peter down.

JANICE leaves.

MATTY feels his bruised chest and back and stretches himself.

PETER arrives.

PETER: The two slags are hissing like snakes.

MATTY: What's new?

PETER: Well…go on…

MATTY: Go on what?

PETER: Say sorry.

MATTY: What for?

PETER: Almost breaking my arm.

MATTY: Bollocks.

PETER: You've changed. You know that?

MATTY: Only playing, Peter.

PETER: I'm waiting…

MATTY: I'm sorry. Okay?

PETER: Now…what do you want me to do?

MATTY: Undress me.

PETER: Okay…later, but…

MATTY: Now! Take my shirt off.

PETER unbuttons the shirt and slips it off to reveal the bruising.

PETER: Christ! When did this happen?

MATTY: Last night. When I got in from the club. He wanted to know where I'd been, so I told him the truth.

PETER: That you'd won the sexy nipple competition?

MATTY: I didn't get that far. I was on the floor getting a good kicking. 'You fucking poof!' 'No queers under my roof!' You know…traditional family values…

PETER: (*Being gentle with MATTY's damaged body.*) Poor Matty. Does this hurt? (*He kisses the bruises.*)

MATTY: I'm not going back. I'll kill him if I get a chance.

PETER: Move in with me. My mam'll look after you. She won't mind. There's a double bed in my room. We can share.

MATTY: It's my mam I'm worried about. Being left alone with that bastard.

PETER: I don't think there'd be room for the three of us.

MATTY: I wasn't thinking that, you prat! Anyway, she's got a sister in Wallsend. She could move in with her. But I need help to move out.

PETER: How much stuff have you got?

MATTY: I needn't take it all. But there's my computers and stereo. And that wind up gramophone. And my dance records. And my videos. And my Newcastle United collection. And my telly. My skateboard. My two hamsters…

PETER: You've still got hamsters?

MATTY: Aye… Shearer and Ginola…

PETER: Ginola?

MATTY: It's a seriously old hamster. My mam could never cope with them. Or my tropical fish collection…

PETER: Hang on a minute…

MATTY: They're really small fish, Peter.

PETER: I bet…

MATTY: The tank's a canny size, mind… I couldn't live without them… I've known then since they were eggs. You've got to help me. I can't stay in that house another night.

PETER: I said you could move in…

MATTY kisses PETER passionately before he can change his mind and starts to unbutton PETER's shirt. They're soon getting physical.

MATTY: Thank you…you've saved my life…we can spend every night together…won't that be wonderful…

PETER: …as long as you don't mind sleeping standing up…

MATTY: …you know I can do everything standing up…

PETER: …and you won't mind if Percy, my pet python, nibbles your gerbils…

MATTY: …you haven't got a pet python…

PETER: ...I think I'm going to need one...

MATTY: ...and my gerbils are dead...ahhh...who said you could lick my prize winning nipples? ...oh...a bit faster...ah...too fast...don't bite...

PETER: ...something's got to gobble the reptiles...

MATTY: ...don't stop...

PETER: ...Robocop should make short work of the tropical fish...

MATTY: Robocop?

PETER: My cat...a deadly serial killer... Oh Matty, I predict years of domestic bliss...providing we're prepared to tolerate the odd massacre...

MATTY: How are we going to move the stuff?

PETER: Hairy Lesley?

MATTY: Would she lend us the van, like?

PETER: Na! She'll drive the bloody thing.

MATTY: We should have kept the rag bags down here.

PETER: Why?

MATTY: Nowhere to fuck in comfort.

PETER: No time for that. You're a business executive.

MATTY: (*Sliding his hands into PETER's trousers.*) Who cares? Let's have a pre-elopement celebration.

PETER: No!

MATTY: Yes!

MATTY slides down PETER's trousers in one skilled movement.

PETER: Bugger off...

MATTY: Do what you're told.

PETER: (*Pulling up his trousers.*) Why?

MATTY: Because…

MATTY uses his strength to wrestle PETER's trousers down again.

PETER: No! (*MATTY takes no notice.*) Not now. For God's sake… Matty…

MATTY: Ummmm… (*Goes down on him, despite PETER's objections.*)

MRS STEINBERG enters in full view of PETER, but MATTY doesn't see her and carries on.

PETER: No Matty…

MATTY: Ummm…

PETER: Matty, please…

MATTY: Ummm… Ummmmmmmm…

PETER slips out of MATTY's mouth, and MATTY sees MRS STEINBERG.

MRS STEINBERG: Thank God something hasn't changed since I left.

MATTY: Welcome home, Mrs S.

The boys get dressed.

MRS STEINBERG: (*Taking in the changes.*) I don't believe my eyes! What have you done?

PETER: Brilliant or what?

MRS STEINBERG: My God, you've been working hard! Where's Karl Marx?

PETER: Matty's been at him as well. He's over there. Quite safe…

MATTY: ...with his friend...

PETER: Matty tossed them off with the steam press...

MRS STEINBERG: That doesn't surprise me.

PETER: Have you had a good time, Mrs S?

MRS STEINBERG: If visiting the graves of five million Jews, including most of your own family, can be described as a good time.

PETER: Sorry, like...

MRS STEINBERG: I'll tell you more later, if you like. Be an angel and bring me a coffee.

PETER: Okay.

MATTY: Is it smart? Are you pleased?

MRS STEINBERG: Someone's moved in next door.

PETER: Not just someone, Mrs S.

MRS STEINBERG: Where are the donations? Where's the junk?

MATTY: All will be revealed!

MRS STEINBERG: Someone tell the girls not to let in any more customers and close the shop. I want everyone down here.

PETER: (*Shouting upstairs.*) Boss's orders! It's a lock out! Down tools, ladies!

MRS STEINBERG: (*Referring to the computer.*) What's that thing doing here?

MATTY: Making money for New Red Flag.

JANICE: (*Off.*) Matty! Furniture van!

MATTY leaves.

MRS STEINBERG: New Red Flag! Don't make me sick.

PETER: Did you like the new sign?

MRS STEINBERG: I hope it's a practical joke.

PETER: It's for real. What about all my painting?

MRS STEINBERG: Astonishing!

PETER: Some of it's still wet, mind.

MRS STEINBERG: I noticed.

PETER: Well…you're not supposed to be here yet.

MRS STEINBERG: Lesley's best wasn't good enough. Dear God, what have you done to my beautiful shop?

PETER: Wait till the others are here. (*Bringing over the coffee.*) There you go, now.

MRS STEINBERG: I'm glad you take staff training so seriously, Peter. I presume Matty is now quite clear what his duties include.

PETER: He's my best mate.

MRS STEINBERG: Really?

PETER: He's moving in with us.

MRS STEINBERG: When?

PETER: Tonight.

MRS STEINBERG: Does your mother know?

PETER: Not yet. She likes Matty. She won't mind. Did Lesley have her van with her?

MRS STEINBERG: Yes. She picked me up from the airport early this morning, bless her. So useful to find someone who can carry six suitcases at once.

PETER: So what have you really been up to?

MRS STEINBERG: Seeing old friends…old comrades…my last time, Peter. I met some relations I didn't know I had. And two old school mates I thought were dead. Those of us that survived…it's incredible how long we've lived…

PETER: You are pleased…you know…with what we've done?

MRS STEINBERG: Later, Peter.

PETER: And you didn't mind what we did with your posters?

MRS STEINBERG: Let me make a confession. I never liked Lenin. My God I tried… I pretended… I read the literature… I studied the history. Karl Marx becomes more obscure the more you read…and Lenin more cruel and cowardly. What I thought they stood for was more important than who or what they were. In the end they became simply icons of faith. But I would never have dared steam them off the wall and roll them up. It took you boys…with your innocent…don't laugh… your innocent view of the world…to see sense and be practical.

PETER: What should we do with them?

MRS STEINBERG: I'll think about that. Now where's the gang?

PETER: I'll see.

PETER leaves MRS STEINBERG alone. She looks at the computer with suspicion. She presses a key and it bleeps 'The Red Flag' at her, to her alarm.

MATTY enters, but the tune carries on, much to MRS STEINBERG's irritation.

MATTY: I've locked the keyboard to stop people meddling. Don't worry. It won't bite.

MRS STEINBERG: Vile machine! How's it making money?

MATTY: Right now, it's taking e-mails and voice messages. Look. There. It tells you. Nothing new in at the moment.

MRS STEINBERG: Where does it say that?

MATTY: There.

MRS STEINBERG: Still can't see.

The others enter.

JANICE: You cannot clear a busy shop just like that, you know.

APRIL: We took another thirty pounds since you came through the door.

PETER: New Red Flag's a success, Mrs S!

MRS STEINBERG: New Red Flag! The next person to say that will be shot!

PETER: Right! We're officially closed for staff training…

MRS STEINBERG: …which is what Peter was at when I arrived…

PETER: …and we've prepared a presentation so you can see what we've done and why we've done it.

JANICE: It's mostly the lads' work…

MATTY: Entirely…

APRIL: …almost…

JANICE: If we'd had our way, things would have gone on as before.

PETER: You've changed your tune now the boss's back!

MRS STEINBERG: Perhaps she knows which side her bread's buttered.

MATTY: Don't put money on it.

PETER: I bet when you stuck the 'Andrew' badge on Matty, you had no idea you were engaging a geek…

MRS STEINBERG: A geek?

PETER: A computer wizard and champion hacker, Mrs S. Anyway… Matty's going to kick off.

MATTY: You gave us five weeks, right?

PETER: And a day…

MATTY: We had no capital to work with. Only what we could make over the counter…about four hundred pounds a week. What was clear to me was that Red Flag was a mess…untidy… inefficient…thieving and scams were institutionalised… everyone was at it, one way or another.

JANICE: Bollocks!

MATTY: We were selling the more interesting donations at well below their market value. We had a narrow view of our territory, seeing most of our customers as living around North Shields. There was no regional ambition, let alone a national or international one. I bought a wind-up gramophone and a bunch of records for a pound. A fraction of its market value. So, for a start, Peter and me…we went to the Business Centre… Peter?

PETER: It's just a hundred yards from the door, Mrs S. We spent an hour there…asking advice an' that…it cost us nothing. She was excellent and they were that pleased to see young lads in…

MATTY: Aye…

JANICE: …and pleased to see the back of you…

PETER: …that they gave us this computer…

MATTY: …which I fixed…it was knackered, like…

PETER: …to get us on line.

JANICE: Now we're out there, shagging in cyber space!

PETER: …and we have a mission statement…

MATTY: …'to make as much money as possible for worthy causes'…

APRIL: They dropped 'socialist causes'. That was them two.

PETER: Too narrow. Anyway, who's to say what's a 'socialist cause' and what isn't?

MRS STEINBERG: That never caused me any problems. Go on…

PETER: We've started writing a business plan, but things are changing so fast, it's difficult to keep up.

APRIL: Do we need a business plan, Mrs Steinberg?

MATTY: If we want a development grant! Don't worry! We'll get something written by next month for everyone to look at.

PETER: This all started in the first week, mind.

APRIL: As soon as you were out of the door.

PETER: If we were going to sell more, we had to get more classy goods in. Waiting for crappy donations to arrive on the doorstep wasn't going to do it.

MATTY: If you haven't got it, you can't sell it.

PETER: So we decided to let Janice have her head…

APRIL: …which we called Operation Aubergine!

PETER: Janice?

JANICE: You know you hated us selling at Tynemouth, right? Well…we've built on that. We have a New Red

Flag stall. We buy off the other traders and sell on. And we've got a deal with Lesley over buying and selling at markets throughout the region.

MRS STEINBERG: What sort of deal?

JANICE: We pay for her transport and she gets a percentage from the shop.

MRS STEINBERG: From here?

JANICE: Yes.

MRS STEINBERG: No way.

MATTY: It's more complicated than that, Mrs Steinberg. I'll be giving you all the facts and figures later so you can study them at home.

PETER: We're doing well out of it, Mrs S.

JANICE: We've also got a gang of scouts who go round all the other charity shops, buying stuff we can sell on at a big profit. And we buy at auctions, house clearances, junk shops…you name it. All those dealers you used to throw out of the shop? They're now on commission from us. We're buying and selling like it was stocks and shares. Sometimes we get it wrong, most times we're right. Our shop manager is April, believe it or not…

APRIL: It's true! I manage the shop…

JANICE: She's still till dipping…shifty cow…

MATTY: Not any more. The till is linked to the computer.

PETER: Matty wrote this programme…

MATTY: …and we're getting CCTV next week.

MRS STEINBERG: Where's the money coming from?

MATTY: From the profits. It's not costing much.

JANICE: Shoplifters hate CCTV, don't they, April?

APRIL: Aye… Now, with this lot flying about all over the place, someone's got to take care of upstairs. That's me. Shop Manager. And we're getting a new 'Andrew' next week on work experience.

MATTY: Another Byker lad.

PETER: Cute bum. Huge dick, Janice.

MATTY: Aye. A right gob-stopper…

APRIL: With all the new stuff coming in, Janice rents the shop next door…

JANICE: …for next to nothing. More than pays for itself…

APRIL: So we've got more space down here in the engine room. Matty?

MATTY: Down here we have access to dealers' lists worldwide on the internet. When we get something worth selling, it goes on our website. In the past two weeks, we've sold goods to America, Switzerland, Japan and Germany. By seeing what other people are selling at, we're learning fast about international prices. But we still need expert advice on books, LP records, furniture, clothes…we sold a dress for four hundred pounds last week, Mrs Steinberg. It cost us a fiver.

MRS STEINBERG: From another charity shop?

MATTY: Yep!

PETER: There's too many people pretending they know what they don't…

JANICE: …and most of them work in charity shops!

MATTY: Their loss…our gain…

PETER: Tell her about scouting classes.

MATTY: We've been training our scouts about what to look for.

JANICE: I'm against that. They'll end up buying for themselves.

MATTY: But we pay them a percentage on what they buy for us, and a percentage on the profit we make. We do the hard bit, the selling.

PETER: While they're better off working for us, they won't want to work for themselves.

MATTY: They've got no overheads. We take the risks.

PETER: Selling for serious money is vital. Any idiot can buy and sell for peanuts. Matty's the key man.

MATTY: And to keep us lot on board, we pay all staff a bonus on sales plus generous expenses. This is just about legal, so it doesn't interfere with other benefits staff are getting from the state.

PETER: So what do you think, Mrs S?

MRS STEINBERG: I'm disgusted. New Red Flag! That just about sums it up. It's a complete betrayal of everything we stood for.

MATTY: I don't see why. Do you want to see the figures?

MRS STEINBERG: Not particularly.

JANICE: You bloody well should!

MATTY: Last week…after bonuses and commissions were paid out…we made four thousand, five hundred and thirty-six pounds and three pence…that's more than twice as much as you used to make in a month.

PETER: We made two thousand pounds on a batch of LPs. You used to sell them for twenty-five pence each.

MRS STEINBERG: Four thousand five hundred pounds profit in a week?

MATTY: Yes. Since you left, we've got about nine thousand five hundred pounds in the kitty for New Red Flag to distribute to 'worthy causes'.

PETER: One way or another, we've got five extra people working for us outside the shop.

MATTY: For themselves, actually, only we get the lion's share of the profit.

PETER: All the other charity shops…they're just amateurs, Mrs S. New Red Flag's the real thing.

MRS STEINBERG: It's a nightmare.

JANICE: Bollocks! It's a miracle.

MRS STEINBERG: How you make money has just as many ethical implications as how you spend it.

JANICE: We're not robbing banks or mugging people on the street.

MRS STEINBERG: I presume you've put up the prices in the shop?

JANICE: Some of them.

MRS STEINBERG: So the working classes are now paying more, thanks to your reforms?

MATTY: Most things in the shop are still incredibly cheap. The serious money is made down here.

MRS STEINBERG: So the shop is really a cover for an international market, operating from the basement?

MATTY: You make it sound sneaky.

MRS STEINBERG: It is sneaky, Matty. And exploitative.

MATTY: I don't get it. We're doing what all the other charity shops try to do, only doing it better. Look at the money, Mrs Steinberg.

MRS STEINBERG: And how are the other charity shops reacting?

PETER: We can't keep them away, they're that curious.

JANICE: …the ones that know who we are…

PETER: …and what we're up to.

APRIL: They get dead suspicious…when we start spending money in their shops…

JANICE: …they assume their prices are too low…

APRIL: …they're getting greedy, an'all…

MRS STEINBERG: And these scouts…how many of the goods they buy for us…and which we pay cash for…are, in fact stolen?

MATTY: None…as far as we know. We have to have receipts for everything.

MRS STEINBERG: And you keep all these receipts?

MATTY: Yes. There's nothing you can teach me about swap shops, Mrs Steinberg.

MRS STEINBERG: Have the police been round yet?

MATTY: No. (*Giving her a folder of print-outs.*) It's all here…what we're doing…how we're doing it…all the facts and figures. Read this, then we'll talk. Okay?

MRS STEINBERG: Who is this monster? He arrives in my shop the morning I leave. A month later, he's running the place!

PETER: Just a Byker boy who loves cocks, Mrs S.

JANICE: Look! We've got to open up the shop again. We should be having this meeting after hours.

APRIL: Costing us money, this is.

MRS STEINBERG: God! You're all infected. Open up! They're queuing round the block by now…

JANICE: Move your arses…

JANICE and APRIL go upstairs.

MATTY: (*Checking the computer screen.*) Messages… (*He gets to work.*)

MRS STEINBERG: (*To MATTY.*) You're a monster with a dirty mouth.

PETER: There's more to him than that, Mrs S. He's a great dancer and my best mate. We're out clubbing most nights.

MATTY: Someone in Taiwan wanting old valve radios…

PETER: (*To MRS STEINBERG.*) Take your time, Mrs S. Read Matty's print-out. Okay?

MRS STEINBERG: Don't patronise me, you randy catamite. (*She settles down to do what PETER suggested.*)

MATTY: Someone in Birmingham wanting Bakerlite… Oh! Mr Faithful in America again! Does he never sleep? This is not a chat line, you bastard. (*MATTY types furiously.*)

MRS STEINBERG: Peter, go and tidy the books. Off you go…

PETER leaves.

MRS STEINBERG: (*Looking up from the print-outs.*) How do they pay?

MATTY: Over the net?

MRS STEINBERG: Yes.

MATTY: Credit card, generally…we're now an authorised online retailer…and they just fill in this on-screen form…with their credit details.

MRS STEINBERG: How safe is that?

MATTY: Nothing is absolutely safe on the internet. They can also send a cheque or a money order, but it takes longer.

MRS STEINBERG: My God! An honest answer!

MATTY: Anyone can nick credit card details.

MRS STEINBERG: How often have you actually sold something that way?

MATTY: Six times so far. The details are in the print out. Valuable items. Thousands of pounds of business. The problem is not the method. It's getting the right things to sell.

MRS STEINBERG: That's where your scouts come in?

MATTY: Right.

MRS STEINBERG: Why don't you jump ship and set up your own business?

MATTY: One day I will. Now I'm still learning. I'm your Young Trainee, remember? And I've got five more months to do.

MRS STEINBERG: If I don't sack you.

MATTY: What are we going to do about a shop manager who nicks from the till?

MRS STEINBERG: You made her shop manager. To me, April is a volunteer.

MATTY: But you know what she's like.

MRS STEINBERG: Yes. In twenty years she's hardly missed a day. She's worth her weight in gold. Of course I know she borrows from the till. Sometimes I get the money back, sometimes not. But I've never paid her a penny. Her debts are written off as a socialist cause.

MATTY: If she does it again, she's not coming back.

MRS STEINBERG: Really? You haven't taken over the asylum yet, young man. Let me be blunt. Yes. You've made an impressive amount of money in a short time. Whether you can keep it up, month after month is another matter.

MATTY: We'll see.

MRS STEINBERG: I predict that once word gets around that this is now a thriving business, donations will dry up. Secondly, by training your scouts, you're creating the next generation of competitors. Don't interrupt… I know you're trying to buy their loyalty with percentages and bonuses. Okay for a while, but then they'll be off. And you'll train the next lot, and they'll be off. And soon the whole place will be swarming with bloody experts like ants on a rubbish tip!

MATTY: Doubt it. None of them are real experts, anyway. More like treasure hunters. And if anyone two times us, they're dead men.

MRS STEINBERG: Liquidated…

MATTY: End of the line. As for keeping the donations going, I suggest we make a point of giving a few large amounts to local causes and get the maximum publicity. Old people, schools, start an appeal for a new kidney machine for the hospital…that sort of thing.

MRS STEINBERG: You're a dangerous little bastard. You'll end up in politics.

MATTY: Right now, I'm worried about how to leave home tonight. I've got to get all my things over to Peter's place without my dad kicking shit out of me.

MRS STEINBERG: I had to leave home in a hurry once. I was even younger than you. I had no passport, no papers.

MATTY: Where from?

MRS STEINBERG: A small village near Kutno in Poland. My father was a drunkard…straight out of a story by Maxim Gorky.

MATTY: Oh… I read that book.

MRS STEINBERG: Good.

MATTY: Thank you.

MRS STEINBERG: Like a fool, my father thought there was safety in numbers and took the rest of the family to Warsaw. I refused. See this scar? That was my father's farewell present to me. My plan was to walk to Danzig and escape by boat. I ended up having to beg, borrow and steal my way through Lithuania to Latvia…walking most of the way. Like you, I also had a fondness for cocks, which saved my life. From Riga, I boarded a ship to Stockholm. I travelled by land to Oslo… Dear God! …some journey that was! Then on to Stavanger…and then to Newcastle by sea. And here I am, old, but still in one piece!

MATTY: And you did all that with no papers…no passport?

MRS STEINBERG: With only my wits, a lot of luck and a wickedly versatile tongue! I blew my way to freedom, Matty. If you want to survive, do you want my advice?

MATTY: Aye…

MRS STEINBERG: Take nothing with you. Travel light. Tonight, leave all your junk behind. If it wants to follow you, it'll find a way. If not, start again.

MATTY: What happened to Mr Steinberg?

MRS STEINBERG: Poor Stanley, he died. His parents were Russian Jews. We married in 1940 in Cullercoats. That's how I became a British citizen. We were walking along Tynemouth beach. He stopped and looked out to sea. He turned to me and said, 'What are they doing to us?', then collapsed and died in front of my eyes, surrounded by seagulls. The tide was coming in, and I was struggling to drag his body…he was a heavy man…away from the water. I ran up to the road for help. When we got back, poor Stanley was bobbing about with a couple of seagulls sitting on him.

PETER enters with some receipts.

PETER: Twister's just dropped off some stuff.

MATTY: How much?

PETER: Fifteen pounds.

PETER hands over the receipts.

MATTY: What cost seven pounds fifty?

PETER: A table lamp…

MRS STEINBERG: No electrical goods.

PETER: …old…nice art deco figure…no it isn't plastic!

MATTY: (*Getting the money.*) What else?

PETER: He thinks they're original 'Winnie the Pooh' illustrations.

MATTY: Pencil sketches? On white, rough-looking paper?

PETER: Yep…

MATTY: They're fakes. They use a colour photocopier. See them all the time at boot sales. There you go. Fifteen pounds plus one fifty commission. (*Typing in the sales details onto the computer.*) Tell Janice to have a word with Twister.

PETER: She's already started on him…she likes the lamp…

PETER leaves.

MRS STEINBERG: How do you know the receipts are genuine?

MATTY: We're getting to know the dealers. We've also got the goods. If anything costs more than a tenner, they have to contact us before buying.

MRS STEINBERG: It's a risk.

MATTY: Of course, Mrs Steinberg. (*MATTY types in a command and reads the screen.*) We've only taken ninety-three seventy-eight on the till this morning so far. Your decision to close the shop cost New Red Flag money.

MRS STEINBERG: So it's my fault? I step through the door and you lose your precious cash?

MATTY: Forget your old working practices. From now on, we never close.

MRS STEINBERG: I think you've forgotten this is my shop! I started it. I sweated blood for it.

MATTY: I know.

MRS STEINBERG: You've gone too far. You're clever. You made some money and I hate it!

MATTY: You'll love giving away the big cheques. You'll get all the credit. You'll get an OBE.

MRS STEINBERG: It's a total sell-out.

MATTY: To what?

MRS STEINBERG: Capitalism! Percentages…bonuses…
dubious expenses…international credit sales…bribery…

MATTY: …haven't bribed anyone yet…

MRS STEINBERG: …dealers…loans…interest…

MATTY: You're flogging a dead horse, Mrs. Your 'strict
socialist principles'…whatever you once meant by
that…didn't do the business. Face the facts…you've lived
your life in pinko fantasy land and it didn't work!

MRS STEINBERG goes to the computer plug.

Don't!

She pulls it out and the computer crashes.

MRS STEINBERG: That makes me feel a lot better.

MATTY: You stupid bitch! What the fuck did you do that for?

MRS STEINBERG: To teach you a bloody lesson, you
smug little creep!

MATTY: (*Plugging in the computer.*) Never crash the machine!
Damn! Now I'll have to run a health check on the
hard disk.

MRS STEINBERG: I hope it's terminally ill.

MATTY: You just cost us more money, Mrs Steinberg.

MRS STEINBERG: Who said you could start that damn
thing again?

MATTY: Oh grow up! (*He tries to see what has been lost in the
crash. She pulls out the plug again.*) For fuck's sake!

MRS STEINBERG: This is my shop. I decide what we do
here and who does it.

MATTY: What are you frightened of, Mrs Steinberg?
You've finally come face to face with world revolution,
and you pull the fucking plug! (*She heads for the door.*)
Don't go yet! There's something else I want to show you.

MATTY passes over to her a few more pages of print-outs.

MRS STEINBERG: Where did you get this?

MATTY: When you left a month ago, you asked us to check
through the accounts.

MRS STEINBERG: That didn't include my personal bank
statements. How did you get your hands on them?

MATTY: I could have hacked my way in, but I would have
needed all the computers at Newcastle College for a few
hours. Instead I used this. (*He waves MRS STEINBERG's
bank card.*).

MRS STEINBERG: (*Snatching it back.*) Where did you
get that?

MATTY: You left it behind.

MRS STEINBERG: How did you get the PIN number?

MATTY: The 'hole in the wall' allows you three guesses.
The most commonly used PIN is zero zero zero zero.
In Newcastle, a lot of people use the phone code zero
one nine one. I put my money on either your Party Card
number, two seven eight nine, or the date of the Russian
Revolution, 1917. Your Party Card won. After that, the
rest was easy.

MRS STEINBERG: You slimy shit.

MATTY: I haven't withdrawn any money. I assume that all
the cash you pay in comes straight from the shop?
You don't have a separate 'Red Flag' account?

MRS STEINBERG: No.

MATTY: I've marked the occasional cheques you pay out to your socialist causes. I did some arithmetic.
You have quite a lot left over, Mrs Steinberg. Useful if you get short, I should think.

MRS STEINBERG: What precisely are you suggesting?

MATTY: Just an observation. That's a huge amount of money to have slopping around in a current account. You'd get far more interest in a Building Society...

MRS STEINBERG: Mind your own bloody business!

MATTY: ...and even more interest if you invest your capital in other ways. If you need advice on how to handle your affairs more profitably...

MRS STEINBERG: I wouldn't come to you.

MATTY: You need help. If the tax man takes a look...

MRS STEINBERG: Don't lecture me, young man.

MATTY: I don't want you to get hurt.

MRS STEINBERG: You want to know the truth? Once your honeymoon period is over, once you've got yourself into a tangle with Health and Safety, with Social Security and National Insurance, then the tax man is going to come along and fuck you all the way back to Byker!

MATTY: I'll come out on top.

MRS STEINBERG: Then your so called friends will stab you in the back and betray you. Loyalty and money don't mix. They fight like cats and in the end money always wins!

MATTY: I'll stay ahead of the game.

MRS STEINBERG: It isn't a game. It's life and death.

Remember… I've proved I'm a survivor. You have only just dipped your toe in the water.

PETER enters.

You should choose your friends more carefully, Peter.

MATTY: Mrs Steinberg doesn't like the world wide web.

MRS STEINBERG: The shop is closing for the rest of the day…now!

PETER: Not again!

MATTY: We can't go on like this!

MRS STEINBERG: And send the staff down at once!

PETER leaves.

MATTY: Christ! I know why your da belted you one!

MRS STEINBERG: And I know why yours kicks the shit out of you!

The others come in. They know something is up.

Is the shop door locked? (*Silence from the others.*) I assume that's a 'yes'.

JANICE: We're trying to run a business here.

MRS STEINBERG: I know! I know!

APRIL: There's people outside wondering what the fuck's going on!

PETER: Some in here, an' all!

MRS STEINBERG: Shut up and I'll tell you! I've read most of this… (*She waves the print-out and dumps it in the direction of MATTY.*) …and I've listened to what our new boy has to say…and I don't like it. When we re-open the shop…hopefully tomorrow morning…things will be as they were. On the same scale…for the same purpose.

JANICE: There's no turning back now.

PETER: What are we going to tell the scouts?

MRS STEINBERG: Tell them what you like. They're your responsibility, not mine.

PETER: Not as easy as that.

MRS STEINBERG: It's clear you've betrayed everything I've believed in, and I'm not standing for it. If that's not good enough for any of you, you can leave…at once. (*When no one says anything.*) Are you all staying?

MATTY: I'm not staying. You've no vision. Everyone here has worked incredibly hard, trying to put your house in order.

PETER: If Matty goes… (*He feels very guilty at betraying MRS STEINBERG.*)

MRS STEINBERG: Janice?

JANICE: I've got the shop next door, haven't I… If you lads want to move in with me, we'll carry on where we left off.

MRS STEINBERG: Not as The Red Flag Charity shop, you won't.

MATTY: We'll be a business, not a charity.

JANICE: The biggest dealers' syndicate in the region…

PETER: …and abroad!

APRIL: Don't get too carried away, Peter.

MATTY: We're already registered as New Red Flag, and we're staying that way.

MRS STEINBERG: Are you hell!

MATTY: Aye. And you can't stop us!

MRS STEINBERG: We'll see about that! April?

APRIL: I'll stay with you, Mrs S. These buggers would sack me the moment anything went missing.

JANICE: Bloody true!

MATTY: What are we going to do with the money we've made?

MRS STEINBERG: Give it to deserving socialist causes.

MATTY: If you object to the way we've made it, you shouldn't touch it.

JANICE: Some of the stuff we've bought…that was with our money. Not everything here belongs to you.

MRS STEINBERG: I'll be fair. Items that belong to you, you can take next door. As for the money, it's all going to be given away, so don't expect to pocket a penny of it yourselves.

PETER: We weren't going to…

MATTY: …apart from our expenses and monthly dividend.

MRS STEINBERG: But I'll let you agree to where it goes, since you made it. And I still want my name back!

MATTY: New Red Flag is out there in cyber space.

MRS STEINBERG: I wish it would bloody well stay there! Red Flag still means something to some of us and you've hi-jacked it.

MATTY: It's you that's kicking us out.

MRS STEINBERG: Start again. Think of something else. Anyway, you can't stay 'new' for ever!

APRIL: Scratch his bloody eyes out, Mrs S!

JANICE: We'll settle this one in the morning. Right?

MRS STEINBERG: To pretend that what you're doing has anything to do with socialism is a fraud.

MATTY: Who cares? The public doesn't see it that way.

PETER: Shut it, Matty!

JANICE: I'll chuck a bucket of water over the pair of you!

PETER: We'll sort something out, Mrs S.

MATTY: Will we?

PETER: Shut your fucking face!

APRIL: I know, Mrs S! We'll call ourselves 'Left Overs'!

EVERYONE: Oh piss off, April!!

MRS STEINBERG: 'New' is tainted as soon as it's uttered. Haven't you noticed?

MATTY: While it works, we'll keep it.

JANICE: Stop playing the tycoon, faggot face!

MATTY: Okay Okay! Mrs Steinberg, I'll sort out the accounts for the last month, assuming you haven't buggered the machine. Janice, is there a phone line next door?

JANICE: It needs reconnecting.

MATTY: Let's get that sorted now. Janice, show Mrs Steinberg what belongs to us. We'll help you shift things later.

JANICE: Come on, Mrs S.

MRS STEINBERG: April, do the till, please.

MATTY: Yep…help yourself…machine's off…take what you want…

APRIL: Piss off, knob gobbler!

MRS STEINBERG: You boys clear up your things. Sorry to lose you, Peter.

PETER: I'll be next door. Coffee and a massage if you want it.

MRS STEINBERG: Byker boy, I want Karl Marx back on the wall before you go. Don't bother with Lenin.

MATTY: Is Karl Marx Baldy or Beardo?

MRS STEINBERG: Beardo. (*Meaning MATTY.*) Watch your back. He's dangerous, this one…

PETER: If he misbehaves, I'll put arsenic on my knob.

MRS STEINBERG: If you want a life, you'll do it tonight…

MATTY: Remember what you said to me on my first morning? Don't be frightened of your own ideas. Think your own thoughts, not someone else's. Good advice, Mrs Steinberg. That's exactly what I've done, and, my God, how you hate it!

MRS STEINBERG: Bad ideas! Bad thoughts!

The women leave.

MATTY: Did the lady say thank you, or what?

PETER: I knew you were trouble the moment you battered me in Byker cottage!

MATTY: She really gets on my tits! We've all worked our balls off to rescue that bitch from the nineteenth century, and she just pisses on the lot of us!

PETER: She's old, man Matty.

MATTY: Just met her face to face for a couple of hours in the whole of my life and the fucking cow's sacked us!

PETER: My mam'll be furious.

MATTY: Mine won't be pleased.

PETER: When we get back to my place, don't say a word, right?

MATTY: We're reorganising…

PETER: No. Say nawt. Let her find out gradually, like. Shit! All that bloody painting…

MATTY: (*Turning on the computer.*) Good practice for what's coming. Let's turn next door into something special.

PETER: Me decorating full time and you playing computer games?

MATTY: Find Karl Beardo and stick him up.

PETER: You're still o'er bossy. Too much gob.

MATTY: And don't you just love it?

PETER: Don't bank on it.

MATTY checks over the computer to see what's lost and whether the website has had any hits.

MATTY: Looks like we've lost some till information. Your fault, bitch. No e-mails. No hits. World, what are you playing at, man!

PETER: (*Trying to hang up Karl Marx with Blu Tak.*) You best go back where you were, pet…

MATTY: We'd have left her anyway. Sooner or later. Business is business. We'll make wor fortunes, Peter

PETER: (*To Karl Marx.*) What do you think? Smart, eh? Progress or what?

MATTY: …you and me…together…we'll travel the world.

PETER: Looks okay there, doesn't he?

MATTY: Peter…

PETER: What?

MATTY: It's been a good day.

PETER: Really?

MATTY: Not over yet.

PETER: Don't look at me like that…

MATTY: Like what?

PETER: Like you missed your elevenses.

MATTY: I was not! Anyway, it's nearer lunch, and you know I like something substantial.

PETER: Well, don't look at me. Are we taking the computer?

MATTY: Bloody sure. Safer here tonight, mind.

PETER: What are we going to do about shifting your stuff into mine?

PETER plays some music on the computer and takes MATTY in his arms to dance.

MATTY: Leave it. Can you lend us some clothes?

PETER: Aye. Ne bother.

MATTY: Me mam'll feed Shearer and Ginola tonight.

PETER: …and the fish…

MATTY: …aye. Anyway, she's spending the evening down at the OK Coral. Wyatt Earp's been oiling his six-shooter all day.

PETER: Fun for some.

MATTY: Shame about Mrs S. I really like that woman.

PETER: You do?

MATTY: Yep.

PETER: Me too…

MATTY: Makes no odds.

PETER: Pity.

MATTY: Our world, not hers…

They dance, differently from the end of Part One, under the impassive gaze of Karl Marx.

The End.